Uncover

Maxine Lorraine

Presentation by *BookLeaf Publishing*

Web: www.bookleafpub.com

E-mail: info@bookleafpub.com

ISBN: 978-93-95784-25-2

First edition 2022

DEDICATION

To my beautiful Harley-James, you will always be the reason. And to Kyle, for pushing me to pick up the pen in the first place. I couldn't have realised this dream without you.

PREFACE

This book is meant to be read little by little, piece by piece in the hopes you find something between the lines that makes you feel less alone.

Throughout this crazy journey of my life I've battled with Trauma, PTSD, Anxiety, Insomnia, BPD, Addiction, Grief, Homelessness, PCOS and Infertility (to name but a few). To say the past few years have been rough would be an understatement, but the one thing I've come to realise is that God will always use every bad thing in your life for your good. Whatever it is you're going through right now -you're actually growing through. And you might not be able to see the reason why you're standing in the eye of this storm today but you will. Trust me.

You will.

Life can be dark and difficult and messy, but you weren't meant to walk through it on your own.

You matter.

Love always,

Maxine x

Girls Like Me

I stand at the tender place
where the ocean strokes the sand
and I beg her
for rest.
To wash away all traces
of lost love
and lukewarm memories,

To erase the harshness
of August
and the floodgates that opened
when she came.

I pray for the moon to will the tides
to drown my ache
and exfoliate
this pressing longing
from my skin.

But the ocean listens
only to the moon
and the moon grants no wishes
for girls
like me.

Things My Mother Never Told Me

That to be her daughter is to be a wound that never heals, that the skin can't knit together if you keep picking at the edges and she never did know how to care for an injury without making it bleed.

That there was a cross attached to my name before I left her womb and I'd spend the rest of my life learning ways to carry it. Some ways are healthier than others and I've chosen the poison every time.

(I guess we aren't so different after all).

She never told me that dreams were meant to be chased. That little girls with smart mouths could rule the world some day, that their imaginations are something to be protected, honed and tended to like my grandmother's garden and all of its blooms.

She said it takes sunlight, water and a whole
load of nurturing to grow a sunflower. The
problem was, my mother couldn't give what she
didn't have inside of her and so I became a
cactus, with a tongue as sharp as my skin.

To be my mother's daughter is to bleed and to
grow thorns and to pray that they don't pierce
the skin of my children after me. To break the
cycle so that the generations to come may never
be bowed under the weight of the same branch.

To be my mother's daughter is to make sure this
ends with me.

Lesson Number One

Know the difference between
giving joy to others
and sacrificing yourself for it.

To Be A Better Person

smile at a stranger / compliment a friend / do
something for somebody else without expecting
anything in return / just to see the curve of their lips
when they smile / because their smile is everything /
because it lights up the folds of your heart / because
life can be heavy but their shoulders don't have to be
/ because you can share the weight / pull back the
curtains when you find them in the dark / because
sometimes all we need is a helping hand to let the
light back in / do something for yourself / create time
and space to really get to know yourself better / dig
deep inside the darkest corners of your soul and pull
whatever you find hiding in the shadows up to the
surface / let the light flood through the cracks of your
aching bones / because you deserve to be free / do the
inner work / figure out why you are the way you are /
call yourself out on your mess / hold yourself
accountable / understand that they're only human /
and you are too / understand that you still have so
much room left to grow and commit yourself to doing
so / remember to put on your own oxygen mask first /
because the people you love deserve the very best
version of you / and you deserve to know her too.

Cutting Ties

I struggled to untangle our roots
because history knotted them together
so tightly
and my soft heart
never wanted to damage yours
in setting mine free.

But I've wilted too long in your shade,
and this time
I must choose me.

Growing Pains

I've been peeling back layers of myself for a while now, like pass the parcel at a kid's party. If I just remove this skin and this one and this one, there'll be a prize at the bottom. There might be something good in there. Something worth holding on to. Something worth keeping. But you see, I've been wearing this mask for as long as I care to remember and I'm scared I won't recognise what I see when it slips; I'm scared I won't like what's underneath all of this.

Let Love In

It takes courage
to give yourself to another,
naked and vulnerable, scars
on full display. Laying yourself bare,
showing the parts of you
that carry the most shame.
Allowing them to hold each part of you,
the parts you feel are the least
deserving of being held.

You can love until you burst, with that big heart
in your chest
but it takes courage,
to let them give you some of theirs.

And I hope you'll find the courage,
I hope you'll be brave
enough to let love find you, to hold you,
because this world can be cold
and the mountains ahead of you are
oh so high,
but it's love that will warm your bones,
that will give you the strength to climb.
It's love,
that makes the view from the top
      the most breathtaking of all.

Grace

I trace the lines of my reflection in the mirror
and wonder
if I'll ever see something more
than an accumulation
of every
mistake
I ever made

Every wrong turn,
every road I wandered,
every word that turned bitter in my mouth
when I realised
I couldn't take it back.

How much longer must i stare at this face
before I learn to stomach it?

How much longer must I look into these eyes
before I realise

they're human.

Forgive Yourself

Forgive yourself for falling short. For taking the
wrong path when trauma skewed your vision.
There's no instruction manual on how to carry
yourself when your world falls apart, so forgive
yourself if your ways of coping have been less
than perfect. Forgive yourself for choosing
temporary relief when the pain threatened to
consume you. You did what you did out of pure
survival and you don't have to hate yourself a
moment longer for it -you've already paid the
price. Forgive yourself for staying too long in
spaces that didn't appreciate the rhythm of your
breathing or the melody of your heart when it
beats. For giving the best parts of yourself to
people who sought out your weakness and
revelled in all they could gain from it. Forgive
yourself for not recognising the difference
between who was praying for you and who was
preying on you. Forgive yourself for your
vulnerability. Love yourself for it, even. it takes
real bravery to lay yourself bruised and bare at
the feet of cynics. Forgive yourself for allowing
their cruelty to get under your skin. For
internalising the words they spoke on your name

instead of recognising them for what they were
-a reflection of their own insecurities. Forgive
yourself for not seeing enough of your worth to
set healthy boundaries. For failing to protect the
little girl inside of you who needed saving. For
not realising that the only person she needed to
come to her rescue was you.

One Pink Line

He takes the stick from my hand,
traces his fingers across my vacant belly
and tells me

"Have faith, it'll happen.
What can the doctors know
that God doesn't?
what is a womb
that He can't fill?"

And i adore him for his optimism
but,
with each caress
of my malfunctioning uterus

the emptiness grows bigger.

Emptiness with a heartbeat,
an eternal gestation.

I miscarry my dreams
onto this cold bathroom floor
and wonder
how many parts of one person can be broken
before they shatter into
pieces.

I Wear My Grief Like A Necklace

cold against my skin
sometimes it chokes me,
buries itself within.

I wear my pain like a wedding gown
heart against my sleeve,
I swear my love as a vow,
the only way I can get it to leave.

I wear my strength like makeup,
the mask I show the world,
I keep my secrets to my chest,
a story forever untold.

It's Not Too Late

To unpack, to iron out the creases, to drop it all off at the thrift store. To start over, to build a whole new life for yourself. You were created by the ultimate creator who gave you the ability to create. The possibilities are endless, nothing is beyond your reach. It's not too late to pour a little magic into your morning coffee; a sprinkle of love, a stir of hope. To turn your tongue popsicle blue, to stick it out at the jerks who'd like to ruin your day. It's not too late to let your inner child out to play, to laugh, to mold the world into something magical like plasticine in your hands.

J'ai déchiré ma chemise pour t'arrêter de saigner

You stood at my door, forehead slick with rain,
holding two broken halves of the world in each
hand   begging me
to take the pieces, to put them back together, to
find a way to mend it. I recognised the pain in
your eyes as my own but I wasn't prepared for
how much deeper this knife would cut. I
couldn't stomach your pain like I could my own,
but that's the thing with pain. It's easier to carry
when it's in the arms of the people who deserve
it. And so of course, I took the shirt from my
back
and wrapped it round your shoulders. Left
myself bare to cloak you, to comfort you,
to fix what I didn't break.

We Delight

We delight in the rainy days.
In the knowing that even the thickest dirt can be
washed away.
That we can be clean.
In knit blankets and fog blankets and all things
that make us feel held.

In the sticky fingers of our children,
their arms around our neck, more precious
than diamonds or gold. In the very essence of
them,
the way their eyes light up with wonder
the crinkle when they smile.
We delight in the way they show us how to see
this world
with awe.

In tending to our gardens, watching the way they
tuck inside themselves,
only to bloom once more.
Planting the seeds of hope,
nurturing them into rainbows of colour
and life. We delight in the beauty of the things
we sprinkle a little love into.
Because love makes all the difference.

We delight in the rise of the sun
watercolours bleeding
the deepest oranges and golds, an ode to
a fresh start, a do-over,
a chance to do better.
We delight in the moon, the way she mothers us
through the dark.
the way she says 'you may not have been able to
see me, but I've been here all along'

And At The End Of The Day

all I can ask of this life
is to say that I have loved
and been loved in return

I'm In My Sunday Best

and I'm thinking of you (again). I'm praying for a bed that doesn't sink under the weight of our memories and for late rises and for poetry that doesn't have your name hidden between every stanza. I'd like to feast on fifty synonyms of the word 'want' without being reminded of you. Devour fifty synonyms of the word 'need' without being reminded of myself after you left.

Is it so much to ask —for my poetry to be mine again? For my bed to be mine again, for the whisper of you to quit haunting all of my favourite places?

I can't help but think of your ghost and the audacity it has to take up so much more space than you ever did. How it moved itself in and unpacked it's things and refused to leave and how ironic it is that you never did the same.

It Will Be Beautiful This Time

I'll pull the sun from the sky with my bare hands
and swallow it whole so my body forgets what
darkness looks like. I will be beautiful this time.
I'll paint my floors yellow and I'll lay on them
and nobody will know where they end and I
begin. Fresh flowers will fill the vase on the
kitchen counter and as they open so will my
heart and i'll remember how to love —in a
wholesome way; no longer weak, nor diluted.

I'm not sure if i ever knew how to accept love in
return or if i believed in its existence at all, but
the sun lives inside of me now and who doesn't
love the sun?

I'll warm people gently with my rays this time,
my beam won't burn.

It will be beautiful this time.

I Hated My Body Less When I Realised I Couldn't Kiss You Without It

Hold you without it. Breathe you without it.
Taste freshly ground coffee or my favourite wine
or pasta with garlic without it.

Couldn't listen to my dad's bad jokes without it,
dance barefoot in the kitchen without it, smell
vanilla bean buttercream candles without it.

Couldn't lick icing from the spoon or curl my
fingers through yours or cry at a sad movie
without it. Couldn't travel to new places without
it, immerse myself in different cultures without
it, feel the sun on my skin without it.

Couldn't read a book without it or smell the
crispness of the pages or lose myself in another
world without it. Couldn't write without it, create
without it, become someone I'm proud of
without it.

Couldn't make a playlist or blast my favourite
song and scream the lyrics in the car without it.
Couldn't watch the sun go down, get drunk,
laugh around the fire talking about old memories
and falling even deeper in love with my friends
without it. Couldn't tell you I love you without
it, that I'm grateful for you without it, that I'm
glad you exist without it.

I hated my body less when I realised that neither
the shape of my tummy nor the dimple in my
chin could ever stop me from experiencing,
feeling, touching, laughing, tasting or knowing
this all encompassing love that lives inside my
bones. I hated my body less when I realised
she's given me so much more than I could ever
give her. she's given me a home and all I ever
gave her was an eviction notice.

You're Beautiful

When you blink your eyes open in the morning, still foggy and clouded with sleep. You're beautiful on the nights you pray by your bedside for morning not to come. When the sadness wraps herself around you and your shoulders sag because this is all so heavy. You're beautiful when the heavens open and the rain pours over your cheeks. When you're sucking in your tummy at the mirror, wondering when and how you gained all this weight. You're gorgeous on your worst hair day. When you haven't shaved your legs in weeks. You're beautiful when the world tells you you're not. When you lose your temper. When you can't understand how they put up with you or why they stay. You're beautiful when your bed feels just too hard to leave, when your clothes are strewn across the floor. You're beautiful when your lipstick smudges against your teeth, when you can't give your eyeliner just the right amount of wing. You're beautiful when nobody notices. Even with your ache, your confusion, your messiness. You're beautiful when you're exhausted but you get up anyway. You're beautiful when you don't. You're beautiful when your face lights up with

hope, when you begin to see the sun again.
When you're doing what you love, what sets you alight. You're beautiful in your oversized tshirt and golden legs, dancing in the kitchen. You're beautiful smoking your fifth cigarette, drinking your weight in caffeine. When you're drunk at 3am sending the text that will probably ruin your life. You're beautiful with every regret, every mistake. Every bitter pill you've been forced to swallow. You're beautiful under the setting of the sun and the brightness of the moon. You're beautiful when nobody says it, when you don't say it. Especially then.

You're beautiful.

A Letter To The Old Me

Oh sweet girl, don't worry. Soon you'll leave this town behind. Soon these people will disappear like wisps of smoke that seep through your fingers but cannot touch you anymore. Soon, you'll come home to the sleepy little seaside town you always daydreamed of and all will be okay. Soon, you'll swim in the ocean and splash with your baby and eat ice cream and you'll wear no makeup and your hair will be soaked and you will feel beautiful. Soon, you'll sleep soundly in your lover's arms. He'll tell you nobody exists in this world except you, and he'll mean it. Soon, you'll lay in on Sundays and have pancakes and coffee in bed with two halves of your heart on either side of you and they'll laugh and make jokes and you'll cry happy tears because you can't quite believe life blessed you this much. You'll live by forests and lakes and you'll take slow afternoon walks with his fingers entwined in yours, listening to nothing but nature's sounds and it will feel like a soothing balm to your soul. Soon, you'll have the chance to take all of the bad things that happened to you and use them to help other people who are going through the same and you'll finally understand why God gave those battles to you. Soon, you'll have clarity on your friendships and a higher standard of how you deserve to be treated and your circle will become very small, but the ones who remain are beautiful and kind and love you dearly, as much as you love them. Soon, you'll read books again and remember how good it feels to smell brand new pages and lose yourself in the words. You'll write. Terribly, and then better and then terribly again but you won't even mind because you enjoy it and it makes your soul happy and it helps your mind to make sense of the ever flowing river of words and times and memories and experiences and thoughts that used to drown you but now spark excitement and curiosity. Soon, you'll hold in your hands a published book with your name on it and won't possibly be able to fathom that you created it and other human beings are reading it and it's yours. Soon, you will love your home again and you will fill it with pretty things and comforting things and things that permeate every fibre of your being with peace and serenity and you'll sleep easy there. You'll gain some weight but that's okay because your face looks happier now and your eyes shine bright again. Soon, the people you thought you'd never live without won't even cross the corners of your mind and you'll be okay with that. Soon, you'll forgive

every one of them, and you'll forgive yourself
too. Soon, you'll value your peace so much that
you refuse to let anyone or anything take you
back to the place you prayed your way from.
Soon, you'll understand why you went through
everything you did. Soon, you'll even feel
grateful for it. Because the places you're going
and the person you're becoming are so, so
incredibly worth it. Soon, this will all make
sense. Soon, it won't hurt the way it does right
now. Just keep a hold, little one. Didn't I tell
you, better days are always coming? And they
are. They really, really are.

Life Can Be Really Fucking Beautiful Sometimes

One day we wake up and see blessings in the chair where pain used to sit. Music reverberates from the walls and sunlight floods through the cracks in the curtains and people smell like kindness and strawberries taste like the summer of 5 years ago. We wear love like perfume and laughter like jewels and we soak in the moments and feel glad that we're here.

Our hearts are full and gratitude seeps from the pores in our skin. We see gifts everywhere we look, and almost all of them are the simplest things that life has to offer. Things people take for granted. Things we've taken for granted. Things we forgot to notice when our hearts were so full of pain that we didn't have room for anything else. But now we see them. Now we see.

Life can be really fucking beautiful sometimes.